Turning Toward Home

Garn Barcud

Turning Toward Home

Mary Perkins

BIBLIOFILES

BIBLIOFILES

Published in the United Kingdom
bookbibliofiles@gmail.com

© Mary Perkins 2016
All Rights Reserved

A catalogue record for this book is available
from the British Library

ISBN 978-0-9571856-1-6

CONTENTS

Dedicated to my friend and mentor
Anne F. Stuck
who helped me see that 'less is more'
and whose friendship I have treasured,
and for Sarah
who loves this land.

ACKNOWLEDGEMENTS

I acknowledge a huge debt to my parents, Arthur and Ann Perkins, both of whom loved poetry and knew how to recite it well. They did so on the many car journeys we took to and from our home in Carmarthen to Pembrokeshire, partly as a way of keeping three some-times restless children quiet. In doing so they gave me a gift beyond compare. My Pembrokeshire relatives gave me the gift of knowing that I too, though raised fifty miles distant, belonged to this land. My hus-band Richard has been a source of constant, patient, loving support, continual encouragement and much-needed technical assistance. Anne Stuck whom I met in Boone in the 1990s was an invaluable mentor for many years, encouraging me to seek publication of my poems. I also am most grateful to Bruce Lader for his continuing sound advice and encouragement. My grateful thanks to my cousin Caroline McLachlan who has lovingly created the cover illustration and drawn the black and white sketches which are included along with these poems, and to Erica Leith for her work on the design and production of the book. My warmest thanks to May Hofman, my highly-skilled editor and dear friend, who loves this corner of Wales,

INTRODUCTION

I was born in Carmarthenshire in West Wales. This land of lush pastures, fish-filled rivers and tumbling streams, woods, wide estuaries and ruined castles was a paradise for a growing child. It is the land of Merlin the magician, for according to local legend, Merlin was born to a nun in Carmarthen Priory. But for my parents, my two brothers and myself, there was another land of greater enchantment some fifty miles to the west, a windswept, almost treeless peninsula called Pencaer on the north Pembrokeshire coast just to the west of Fishguard. My parents and theirs were born and raised either on the headland itself or nearby, as were generations of both families before them. My parents felt the longing for their home all their lives, while they lived and worked, all their married life, in the neighbouring county. I have felt the pull of North Pembrokeshire all my life, wherever I have lived and worked.

This headland lies in the land of St David, the patron saint of Wales, who lived and taught here in the sixth century. His followers established many of the small stone churches that dot the landscape. In the twelfth century the Normans raised a breath-taking cathedral dedicated to St David.

It is also a land rich in prehistoric remains. It is the fabled land of the Mabinogion, the name given to the first English translation of a collection of medieval Welsh legends which draw on pre-Christian Celtic mythology.

Here you can walk the Pembrokeshire Coast Path, a public footpath one hundred and eighty miles long which follows the coastline right around the county through some of the most spectacular coastal scenery in Britain. This coastal land lies within the Pembrokeshire National Park, one of only three such national parks in Wales. It is also the place where most transatlantic jets heading for Heathrow and Gatwick now make landfall over Britain.

Eiluned Lewis, a Welsh writer whose mother's family had deep roots in the St David's area, has written of it in these words: 'this country casts a spell on strangers, and holds the natives in so fast an enchantment that they cannot escape it, all their lives long, so much is it in their blood, pervasive as the milk-mild air and the all-conquering sea'.

The landscape of North Pembrokeshire and the people I have loved, whose lives were so deeply intertwined with this particular corner of Wales, are the inspiration for most of the poems in this collection. The reader will find some notes at the back of the book which I hope will help those who may find the occasional Welsh place-names baffling. I have added to these notes a little historical information about some of the places mentioned in the poems. Three of the poems, 'Swift', 'Requiem' and 'Voices', are set in Carmarthenshire. One poem, 'Manorbier', is set in South Pembrokeshire.

PRESELI

West of Cross Hands
as the road rises
to breast a ridge
on a clear day
I look to the horizon
for that distant smudge
of low blue hills,
Preseli,
backbone of that
lovely, westward land
and my heart rises
knowing that up ahead
there is still
a small wildness,
home to the stonechat,
the ancient, tumbled rocks
and the agile, scrawny
Preseli sheep.

And I rejoice
that I am hefted
to that land
as surely as
those sheep are
to their hills
and though I live
three thousand miles
away where my days
are full and happy,
it is with the deepest
of my heart's content
that I turn towards home.

FESTIVAL DAY

Today we walked from
Garn Barcud to Pwll Strodyr.
Shags on black rocks
in a restless green sea
lifted and closed and
lifted again their
glistening wings.
We ate our lunch
at the waves' edge
and walked home,
small figures in this
wondrous landscape
of sea and cliffs,
shingle beaches,
sheep-filled fields
and widest sky where
slowly-moving clouds
stippled the waves with
ever-shifting shades of
purple, indigo and blue.

While it is yet light
we sit in the house
of Dewi Sant, hushed,
expectant, as the conductor
raises his arms and his baton
and this ancient, glorious place
fills with such wondrous sound
that surely the saint himself
comes back to listen.

The long summer day
fades into night as, brimful
of sea air and music, we follow
the coast road home and
we lie close under the
slanting cottage roof

sighting the North Star
through our small skylight
and glimpsing Ursa Major
sail across the ocean of the sky.

St David's Head

PENMAEN DEWI / ST DAVID'S HEAD

In the misting dampness
of this late Spring day
we follow the familiar path
from Whitesands, past
St Patricks's ruined chapel,
out along the cliff edge
towards the headland.
We pause at the gaunt
cromlech, ponder the stone
circles, clamber over ruins
of defensive walls and
iron age hut circles to
perch on the outermost
rim of the headland,
beyond which, Ptolemy wrote,
there are dragons but today
there is only a quiet, grey,
mist-wrapped sea and
the swirl of currents
below us.

IN NONA'S GARDEN

This garden, sheltered
within these ancient walls
brims with summer warmth
while the westering sun
spills yet more gold
into this bowl of peace.
Bees, laden with pollen,
drone in bumbling ecstasy
in creamy hollyhocks
growing in dark, loamy earth
that surely has been tended
for a thousand years.
Wood pigeons strut and croon
on the great west wall of the house
of Dewi Sant while below them
the Alun quietly sings
its way to the sea.

Was it here, on this level ground
that the saint and his disciples
raised their beehive huts?
Is that only the stream splashing
or if I turn might I glimpse
a barefoot, brown-robed figure
gathering herbs for the saint's supper?

FROM PEN ANGLAS

Lovely lies the land.
Rooted in wood and pasture,
the gentle contours of Preseli
drowse in summer's sun.
Yet lovelier lies the sea.
At land's edge, wavelets embroider
in white lace the tawny, barnacled
and limpet-studded rocks.
Seals rest in still, clear water.
From the cliff's edge we can almost feel
the texture of pebbles beneath them.
Beyond the intricate dance
of white lace on the rocks,
azure and turquoise shade
into a vivid, astonishing blue.
The ocean is a wide and shining water
from Carreg Gwastad to Cemaes
and far out towards Ireland,
a shimmering lake shot with
glints of silver and gold,
and skylarks sing over
the ruins of Crincoed.

AT ABERMAWR

Only a pebble
to tell
of the sea's
gentle swell –

I would bring you,
if I could,
this gentlest of
summer days,
shingle warm
against my back,
horizon merging
in haze,
the waves
lazy tipping
and murmured
retreat.

But I can bring
only a pebble
to tell
of the sea's
gentle swell.

THE APPLE TREE

I felled the tree you planted,
Great-uncle Harries.
It was time –
ready to split it was
in the next autumn gale,
barren, too, though its neighbour,
that you planted also, thrives.

A late, sweet plum I chose
to take its place.
There is such blossom
on its sturdy limbs
and primrose
blooms around it
like spilled cream.

Of course, it's
far too small,
as yet, to fill
the gap; and what
does surprise me
is how much I
miss that gaunt
and haggard shape.

Dinas from Goodwick

ARRIVING AT ISLAND FARM

The train glides smoothly in
almost to water's edge.
The cliffs are a dark curtain.
Moonlight spills silver
on the waves and
the train spills out its
handful of passengers
into this February night
and I amongst them am caught up
and hugged and whisked away
in the rattling Land Rover
which smells so comfortingly
of straw and binder twine and sheep,
to a late supper and a warm bed
and a long sleep from which
I wake to daylight and the sound
of milk pails clanging in
the dairy below.

WINTER DAY AT ISLAND FARM

Cabin-fevered,
under lowering skies,
I launch from kitchen doorstep,
breath whipped sideways
and scuttle, crab-like,
clutching a meal sack
up the wind's tideway,
then slide and tumble
into the sheltering cwm.

Here, in the hollow where the stream runs,
the breakers are a muffled booming
and treetops fight the gale.
Here, in the hushed eye of the storm,
I can gather kindling,
the shipwrack of many winters,
oak, ash and sycamore,
alder and willow,
short, light and brittle,
they will flare into
quick, bright flame.

Meal sack filled, I linger,
lean on a slender beech
and feel in her shifting bones
the tug of distant tides
and see in the winter carpet
the snowdrops'
piercing shoots
of sudden green.

IN MUTE PRAISE

Barefoot at my bedroom window,
I marvel at this March morning –
the sun rising behind Fishguard,
sifting its way through cloud and mist,
in pastel shades of blue and grey –
soft as a dove's breast feathers –
till the palest, most delicate
sunlight spills over the
still, dark waters of the bay.

The ash trees below my window,
back lit against the sunrise,
lift their stark, bare, intricate
tangle of storm-worn branches
in mute praise.

Aberbach headland

SPRING GORSE AT ABERBACH

Grey is the sky and the sea,
brown the rain-filled stream
churning in noisy tumult
through grey boulders
to the shore.

The only sounds are
the tumbling stream,
the cream-lipped waves
scouring the sand and
the cry of oyster catchers
scudding across the bay.

The blackthorn has not woken
from its winter sleep but
the gorse is blazing all
along the headland in
new-bloomed, rich, thick
tapestries of fiercest gold,
cradling in its tight-held,
multitudinous, fragrant blooms
the sweetness of the coming
summer's sun.

MORNING AT PENRHIW

It rained in the night. It stormed
and it blew through keyholes,
down chimneys and curtains flew
like streamers into the room
and trees made a long, loud moan.

Then, at dawn, a sudden quiet
and a blackbird calling through the
darkness of this curtained room.
I would send you this sudden quiet
after the storm.

I would send you many quiet joys,
the splinters of a broken morning wave,
a seagull winging over new-ploughed land,
the scent of deep-drenched violets in the lane
where cows come cruising, dewy-nosed
at milking time.

This golden gorse I'd send to light along your days,
the lark's uprising trill, the bubbling, tumbling
curlew's song – his summer is so short a space of days
in the cold, windy year, while daylight lasts
he cries aloud his sorrows with his joys.

These gorse-lit days and weeks I'd send,
these primrose trails of evening in the west,
the last light on the moor and hedge and hill
and quiet nights we sleep, riding at anchor,
under a quiet moon.

AT GARN MEINI

When I reach these rocks,
this tumult of debris
spewed out
by a red-hot earth,
I wonder,
did Thor wander
too far south?
And I find myself
looking over my shoulder
for the men who so
reverenced these rocks
and who, somehow,
unimaginably,
transported rock
from these hills
to Salisbury plain,
for it seems that
they have only now
set down their tools
for a Bronze Age
tea break and
will be back directly.

HIRAETH/LONGING FOR HOME

We'd planned to be in Wales this week –
though it is lovely here –
in this Virginia night,
fragrant,
rain pattering in treetops,
your breath, sleep-warmed,
beside me while owl
quarters the woods.
Yet this persistent longing
is gnawing in my bones
for sheep-bleat
on Garn Ingli's slopes,
sparse, springy turf
and the smell of the sea.

THE FIRST OF FEBRUARY

No sound on the hillside but the sharp
trilling of a wren breaking the silence
and the distant mewing of gulls.

Nothing stirs the dry bracken,
not a breath of wind moves the pale
winter grasses held in a spell of sunlight.

Then a cry shatters the quiet –
a trembling but insistent cry,
the first cry of a newborn lamb.

In his lair among the tumbled rocks
a fox pricks up his ears, licks his lips
and waits for darkness.

Approaching Penysgwarne

PENYSGWARNE

Behind my eyelids
stand the hills of home.
Breasting Henner ridge,
I watch them rise –
Garn Falch
Garn Fechan
and Garn Fawr.

Though half a world away,
I trace those lovely lines,
dark silhouettes
etched in gold
against a sunset sky,
and beyond, the curving lip
of Bwch Ddu's cliff
rearing high and
plunging sheer
into the sea.

Below Garn Falch
Penysgwarne dreams
woven in storm-sculpted
sycamores, cradled by rooks.
The white gate, open,
glimmers in the dusk.
I turn into the drive
and hear rooks rustling
and grumbling in their sleep
and cattle moving softly in the meadow
beyond the winding beech hedge,
tearing at dew-drenched summer grass.

And I remember how,
rushed in by jet and train,
we wallowed in that meadow grass
among astonished cows
and felt beneath our weary,
jet-lagged bones,

the stubborn outline
of an older, far more ancient
home and we were glad
that men and women
long, so long ago,
had found this place
beneath these hills,
these rocks, these stones
to build and grow.

HOMECOMING

For Aunt Nesta

The tail-lights of the taxi vanish
down the drive and for a moment
it is very dark. I breathe in a deep
draught of rain-washed, sea-soaked
air, hear wind roiling in the
sycamores, chestnut and beech
that shelter this old house.

Then you swing wide the heavy door
that always scrapes along the floor
and whose large, ancient key you
have lost long ago and the familiar
fragrance of this house and the spirits
of all who have cherished it
welcome me in.

I was neither born nor raised here.
My mother did not like this house
and died before she had to live here.
It was too cold, she said, always
draughty. Yet it is my true north,
the place my spirit turns to
moments before sleep.

I know how lamplight falls on
faded carpets, on ancient chests
carved from oaks that were felled
four hundred years ago. I feel
the smoothness of the slender
banister and the rough place
where it was broken and splinted
long before I was born. I hear
the creaks of those wide, shallow
stairs, savour the tock-tick-tock
of the grandfather clock on

Penysgwarne

the landing where through the
tall lancet window I can see
rooks settling in to sleep.

Was it Canada, Denmark
or North Carolina
I had flown from?
I cannot recall but
I can see you
elbowing open
the dining room door
bearing in a supper tray.
Scents of the winter garden,
leeks, parsley, Jerusalem
artichokes and the chicken stock
you have simmered for days
mingle with the fragrance of the logs
sputtering quietly in the hearth
while the windows rattle gently
as the wind tries to nudge its way in.

I have learned with your passing
that houses change when people
who have loved them die.
But there are moments
nothing can erase –
that moment of turning
to see you carrying in,
so very carefully,
that supper tray,
the fragrant soup,
thinly-sliced and buttered
bread, an apple for each of us,
– then you on your favorite stool,
close to the fire, peeling your apple,
tossing peels and core into the
flickering embers, recounting news
of family, neighbours and friends –
moments to savour.

MESSENGER OF LIGHT

'Look, look!' you cry.
'Look at the beautiful white bird!'
reaching with both hands
towards the window
from the armchair where
you have been marooned
these many months,
your eyes clear as water,
gestures eager as
a three-month child.

It is a seagull
tilting past the window
where raindrops hammer
in a Pembrokeshire gale.

You, who through more than ninety years
have tramped so many clifftops,
watched choughs, oyster-catchers,
cormorants, guillemots,
razorbills, kittiwakes, fulmars,
shearwaters, puffins,
gannets diving off Strumble,
peregrines, even once
a hoopoe on Penysgwarne lawn.
Yet this lone, tilting seagull
brings such joy,
this messenger of light.

I PLANTED YOU A GARDEN

For Aunt Nesta

I planted you a garden in the Fall,
remembering you
gloved and aproned,
hunkered down
on a doormat in the
long, curving border,
tussling with weeds
into the bat-dipping dusk,
seeing you tramp,
wellington-booted,
into the kitchen
a gale at your back,
and in your cupped hands,
triumphant,
Christmas roses
or the first spring twigs
of pussy willow.

This mountain winter
has been the hardest,
this spring the slowest,
coldest that we can recall.
The bulbs emerge through
frost and snow and late
in March I peer down
at a thrusting shoot
trying to remember
what it might be
and as I look
it bursts
beneath my eyes,
unfolding its elegant self
into a small iris
and laughing in delight
I think I hear you
laughing too.

THE WIND'S SONG

The wind on the moor is singing to me.
Rushes sway like the waves of the sea.
Cotton grass is dancing. A breeze
rustles the leaves of the willow
where a solitary robin sings.

The blackberries are sour
under a watery August sun.
But I wander from clump
to clump, listening
for that deeper note
of burdens carried
generations deep
on this stony headland,
of chapped hands
and wind-bitten faces,
horse-sweat, harness jingling,
and the thud of hooves
lifting the acid soil.

And of a sudden desolation.
Where life was looked for –
a husband weeps,
a puny newborn
slipping away
is slapped into
motherless life.

The child grows
and marries
and loses
a first-born,
infant son.
The grief compounds,
and is gifted,
with the horses
and the salt-whipped acres
of yielding, patient earth.

GRATITUDE

For my parents

You gave unstintingly,
showered on us
love and safe-keeping,
sacrificed to provide
the best education
that you could afford,
worked and worked
till debts were paid
and we were grown,
and, best gift of all,
you gave us freedom,
let us go.

You cradled us in poetry,
warmed us with rich tales
of relatives long gone
until we felt we knew them,
each and all,
enkindled in us
a deep love of Wales
and a passion for that
bleak and windswept headland
where you both were raised,
a love so strong that when
on summer nights I stand
outside our kitchen door
listening to wind surging
in locusts and white pines,
I hear instead the breakers
beating on Pen Bwch Ddu
and feel myself buffeted
not by this warm, soft
Carolina wind but by
the sweet, salt spray of home.

Llanwnda Church

THERE ARE NO PHOTOS

There are no photos of your wedding.
It was a day of chill and pelting rain,
the sixth day of the darkest month
in a bleak year. Llanwnda church
was cold, her ancient stones
unheated in war or
any other time.

You honeymooned in Ludlow
and woke on the first morning
of your lives together
to news of the bombing
of Pearl Harbor.

SWIFT

Stranded
on my counterpane
a young swift
cannot stir,
its tiny legs
useless in this
new dimension.

I reach gently
in wonderment
to lift him
in cupped hands
towards the window.
He grips my finger
and launches from it
into the sunlight
to fly high
above the winding
loops of Towy,
above the
heat-hazed town.

Fly high, small swift,
fly far and high,
away from this house
of sickness where
I am, by love
and duty bound.
Fly for me also,
small swift.
Fly far and high.

GRIEF

Through this black night
rain fall in sheets.
So beats this new-lodged grief
upon my heart.

Through this black night,
dry-eyed, bone-weary,
I chase sleep.

At dawn
the sodden grasses
trail my legs.
The sparse turf
streams tears
onto dark rocks beneath.

A solitary seagull
keens in flight
and the sea – how it weeps –
in glass-green, heaving rollers
under the sullen sky.

It seems this whole world weeps
but I cannot.

TO MY MOTHER

With all these gifts,
why is it now, at sixty,
I find myself striving
for another birth?

Last night I dreamed
that I went home
and found no
recognizable landmarks but
concrete and shopping malls
where there should have been
heather and gorse-clad hills.

And I remember
that you said to me,
tearfully –
this headland is full of ghosts
and all the people
that I loved are gone.

And I remember how,
once we were grown beyond
the joys of A. A. Milne,
Lewis Carroll, Edward Lear
and Peacock Pie,
you always chose
the saddest poems to recite –
The Lady of Shallot, Œnone,
The Passing of Arthur, Dover Beach –
how underneath a thin veneer,
you were brimming with unshed tears.

Was I the only child of three
who sensed your griefs and fears?
Was I the only one
who felt my father
taut with his own sorrow and
hating to see anyone cry?

You must, you told me,
let your children go,
hold them and you'll lose them.
Let them go and they'll come home.

But there were deeper, tighter bonds
you could not break.
my brothers, busy as bees,
never, I think, noticed.
It is these bonds
I strive to loosen.
It is hard, slow work.
I flail like a creature
caught in murky
depths of kelp,
straining
for sunlit water.

I wake
in the small hours,
hands taut,
weeping
and afraid.
But slowly
I am learning
to open,
with stiff,
cramped fingers,
this sorrowful
ancestral heart,
that I may
break free
and rise,
unencumbered,
towards light.

REQUIEM

For my father

Softly,
with tenderness,
they sing you home,
bare-headed, black-coated
farmers, weathered faces,
calloused hands and
voices like angels' wings,
lifting this bleak crematorium
to the gates of heaven, their
music tumbling about us
in waves of love and loss,
as the sea breaks
on a shingle bank,
rising and falling
and rising and
breaking again.

From seventeen
into your seventieth year
you walked their fields and hills,
shared bread and laughter,
story and song,
nurtured so many hopes
and dreams,
delighting in
their careful husbandry.
In times of pestilence
you wept with them
for cherished,
slaughtered herds.
Nothing,
you once told me,
so wrung your heart
as did the sound of cattle
with foot and mouth,
struggling to breathe.

And every summer
at the grand parade
of cattle, sheep and pigs,
your mellow tones
rolled out across
the grassy show ring
of this lush valley land
in rich doxologies of praise
of men and beasts.

Now it is their turn,
though so many
you have loved
are gone before,
but still the music
lifts us up
on angels' wings.

FOR MY FATHER

The first chill snap of Fall is on us
and leaving for work, you reach
for my father's jacket –
the one you have worn
these thirteen years –
before the winter bites.

Outside the kitchen door
calendulas are still blooming
but the white pine needles
are drifting down
and I feel, beyond them,
the cold of that February,
a gale rattling the windows
and how we lurched about
that house deprived of our
mooring, my cat I had left
with him, so forlorn beside
the empty armchair, he tried
to climb into the grate as
I coaxed a reluctant flame
into damp kindling.

I found his jacket
where it always hung
under the stairs,
stiff with mud,
reeking of cow dung.
I washed and rinsed
and washed and
rinsed again, mended
the rips, sewed on the
missing buttons, brought
it all this way for you.
You said it smelled of cows.

And I recall the sweet security
of his return each evening,

the kitchen door swinging wide,
as in he would come, shrouded in
a bulky mackintosh, so heavy
a child could scarcely lift it, laden
with rolls of maps and plans and
a thick, leather briefcase.
He wore muddy, high-laced
boots and leather gaiters,
britches, a jacket with
leather patches
at the elbows,
and waistcoat, all
of Harris tweed,
barbed-wire proof,
no longer made on Harris,
pockets bulging with pipe
and tobacco pouch,
surveyor's tape, paper clips,
a jumble of elastic bands
around his left wrist, ever
ready for the swift securing
of plans of farms and streams,
woodland and moors and
in his waistcoat pocket
sharpened pencils and
the spare, white handkerchief
he always carried for a needy child.

'Don't cry, don't cry' he'd say
even as he reached for it.
But I will cry now,
for thirteen years are nothing
in a love so rich and deep.
I will keen like the loneliest of gulls
launching across a bleak and wintry sea,
for the smell of cold cow sheds
and the warm breath of cattle,
for the rasping of a calf's rough tongue,
the whickering of ponies,
the welter of sheep milling
and the contented grunting of pigs,

for the rich Welsh voices
of farmers and drovers,
for the lush Welsh fields
of my childhood
and for my father
as you leave the house
in that jacket that
no longer smells of cows.

FIELDS OF GRASS

Wherever there are fields of grass
And sleek cattle tearing at rich clover,
I see you amongst them, smiling slightly,
hands in pockets, cap pushed back,
measuring the depth of udders
and the straightness of backs,
drinking in the sight of them.

Wherever there are oats and barley
ripening to harvest, I see you
leaning on a field gate,
soaking up their promise.
Wherever there are sheep
smoothing the winter pastures,
I see you clambering up
a steep stone hedge
for a closer look.
Wherever there are saplings
you have planted,
struggling up through rush and bracken,
I see you tending them.

Wherever there is laughter
at a tale well told
by resonant, Welsh voices,
I hear yours amongst them.
Wherever there is poetry recited
with splendour and thunder
of colour and wonder,
I hear your strong, warm tones
and I am home.

AT FISHGUARD HARBOUR

You are not on the platform,
nor have you been
these fourteen summers,
yet you are more present to me now
than this whole trainload of passengers.
Easing my way past backpackers
and tourists, Ireland-bound,
seeing only your dear face
scanning the carriage windows,
watching it light up at sight of me,
break into a smile and
a thousand crinkles of welcome
and, forgetting baggage,
hurling myself
at your slight, bony frame.

And I remember
what I did not know
would be the last visit,
leaning from the window
as the train picked up speed,
watching for a final glimpse
as figures on the platform
shrank out of sight.

But in my dreams
you are walking toward me,
illumined with joy.

GRANDMOTHERS DANCING

My mother and my grandmothers
are dancing on the lawn
    My great-grandma's and their mamas
      Are skipping in the barn.
My aunts and great-aunts, near and far,
are waltzing round the corn.
    My cousins, once to thrice removed
    have left the bees to swarm.

They have congaed from the kitchen,
They have polkaed round the yard,
    causing hens and ducks to flutter,
      pigs to snort and then to splutter,
Geese to scatter, calves to skitter,
Left their butter-churns to mutter
    and the mutton broth to sputter,
    shed their bonnets and their shawls,
Their laced-up boots and overalls,
Thrown their clogs over the walls,
    They've unpinned their long-tamed hair,
    twirling, spinning in the bright, fresh air.

O my dear mama and grandmamas,
great-grandmamas and aunts and all
    have unpeeled their woollen stockings
    and are paddling in the duckpond
squeezing mud between their toes.
They've tossed their worries to the sky,
    Hung their huge rage and grief to dry
    And they've laughed until they cry.

JONATHAN

All day you steadfastly
resisted diversion,
strained to wrestle with doorknobs,
clambered onto windowsills,
daubing the glass with
small, sticky fingerprints.

All day it rained,
a drenching summer rain,
lashing the sycamores
into a frenzy, rattling
the seaward windows.

At last you slept,
tear-streaked, spread-eagled
amongst the Sunday papers.
At milking-time you stirred –
perhaps the silence woke you –
the rain had stopped.

Out we swarmed
into that milk-mild air.
We heard the calves
bellowing for their evening feed
and a wind came from the sea
over the moor and
under the stone arch
where damp pigeons preened.

You leaned
into that sweet, soft wind
and found,
to your delight,
it held you up
and there you swayed
laughing in joyous buoyancy
even as the sycamores
dripped huge raindrops
in your hair.

FOR SCOTT

Friend and gifted healer

Friend of my heart –
this was but the latest
of your many gifts –
bidding farewell
to the husk of your soul,
so still in the flower-strewn
bed and our tears falling
as the seemingly endless
falling of rain in this long,
cold spring and summer.

The lilies have drunk their fill
and are bursting in lemon and gold.
The river beyond the brilliant grass
is flowing swift and full, eager
to quicken this long-parched land.

The night you died I wept
as I had never wept before –
I had not known till then
that grief could be so raw,
so fierce, tearing at cells
that had so long resisted,
ripping at tissues I had
not known existed deep
in my heart's core.

After the wakeful anguish
I slept and dreamed
I was riding a strong, black
horse back to the farm, just
visiting and leaving again,
still in the saddle.

Now I am heading home,
flying above thunder heads

north of Charlotte, tracing
the east coast in the fading
light, heading for Wales,
the farm and the headland.

And I know that you
will be there, quick
as the stonechat
darting ahead of us
in the hedgerow,
pivoting with the plover
over the sheep-spotted fields,
your long stride crossing the heather,
lithe, lean and alert now,
the gorse and the brambles
and boulders no hindrance
on the rocky descent
to the sea.

And I know that the fruits
of your life will flower
in all of our lives,
graced and gifted
as we are, by your
deft touch.

LEAVING

I have walked to the land's edge
at daybreak,
finding mushrooms
in the sheep-cropped grass
and spiders' palaces
in the fern.
I have clambered
down chill rocks
to the pearl-grey ocean
and watched fresh colour
wash back into the world.

I have slept in the noontime heather
to the murmur of bees
above a surf-bound bay.
Seals bask in the breakers,
choughs soar in the updraft,
cliff shadows fall through wet sand
till the seas break over the sky.

And when at last I turn inland,
the stubble-fields of brown and gold
are filled with setting sun
and in the dusty hedge I find
a late, late violet,
a sprig of honeysuckle
and the first ripe blackberry.

THERE ARE POEMS

There are poems
that wake me at night.
Next morning they clamour –
write us now – before you
wash dishes. Remember
the peregrine on the Porthgain
cliff top, only feet from us,
plunging its beak into
fresh-caught pigeon,
feathers flying landward
while a lobster-boat tossed
and pitched below in
steep, green seas. Write
of the swallows skimming
out of rising sea-mist at
Penmaen Dewi, and seeming
to pull the summer behind them
and have you forgotten
that Easter Sunday, over
thirty years ago, when, alone,
at Garn Barcud, newly-gifted
to you, after hours of scrubbing
you slept among primroses and
woke to the swish of a buzzard's
wide wings close above you, banking
steeply away, having mistaken you
for a strangely-clothed dead sheep?

VOICES

Hardy wrote of the family face.
It is the voices I recall,
Griffith voices, rich,
mellow baritones,
voices that have
down the centuries,
rung out across rick yards,
reached to the roof timbers
of country chapels,
competed with the winds and waves
on sloping decks of wooden sailing ships,
voices that in welcome warm you
to the ends of your toes.

Muted now, down fifty years
and across three thousand miles,
I hear them as I heard them
at ten years old, hesitating
in the draughty Tanylan passageway
that smelled of terriers and pipe tobacco,
hand on the parlour doorknob, the
fluting tones of aunts and my mother
behind me in the kitchen,
the boys gone swiftly from tea table
to cowshed and barns
and I, the only daughter of two families,
listening to those deep, slow, Sunday voices,
rising and falling in lovely cadences,
pondering the price of in-calf heifers
at Carmarthen mart, analyzing,
the merits of Llanelli's new scrum-half,
musing on Wales' chances in the Triple Crown,
voices that sang and still sing to me
like the quiet chimes
of well-tuned, beautiful bells.

MANORBIER

Of all the different parts of Wales, Dyfed with its seven cantrefs, is at once the most beautiful and the most productive. Of all Dyfed, the province of Pembroke is the most attractive. And in all Pembroke the spot which I have described is most assuredly without its equal. It follows that in all the broad lands of Wales, Manorbier is the most pleasant by far. You will not be surprised to hear me lavish such praise upon it, when I tell you that this is where my own family came from, this is where I myself was born. I can only ask you to forgive me.

Giraldus Cambrensis, 1188 A.D.

Small wonder
that you loved this place –
this curving, westward-facing
sandy bay sheltered from
north and east by gentle hills
your home – the castle –
seemingly rooted in
warm, red rock between
the 'never-failing streams'.

Small wonder
we remember you,
Giraldus, princely son
of Wales and Normandy,
priest, scholar, chronicler,
counsellor to your king,
advisor to an archbishop,
teacher, tutor, chaplain,
traveller and marvellous
teller of tales.

We have forgotten
the name of the Dutchman
to whom King Henry gave
St David's holy see,
for which you longed and strove,
scorning three other bishoprics,
rushing twice to Rome to plead
yours and Wales' cause,

crossing the Alps in winter,
robbed, thwarted, imprisoned
by the King of France on
your way home,
returning bankrupt,
skeleton-thin, a scarecrow,
it is said, with bushy eyebrows.
– and all in vain –
shaking the beloved dust
of Dyfed from your feet,
dying in distant Lincoln,
writing to the end, denied
even your request
for burial at St David's.

We have forgotten,
if we ever knew it,
your warrior brother's
name, his effigy worn
and crumbling now
in the cold church
where you wept for him.
But your words are still
warm with love of learning,
love of country and the sweetest
love of all for this your home.

And if the centuries were
suddenly to slide apart
and you were to come upon us,
bone-weary, saddle-sore,
urging on your tired horse
the last mile home,
clattering through this gateway,
refusing indignantly to buy
admission into your own home,
reining in your horse
in mute bewilderment.
No servants here, not even a
groom to catch your horse's head –
tourists instead – grandparents
dozing on the sun-warmed benches

in this courtyard bright with flowers,
toddlers running and tumbling
over the short, mowed turf,
small boys rushing up and down
the steep, stone steps to the chamber
where you were born,
whole families atop
the gateway towers
that your brothers built

I like to think that, after the first,
sharp daze of shock, you would
slide from the saddle, clap your
long, bony hands to summon
young and old, settle your dusty
robes about your knees and
sitting on the grass,
tell one and all the tale
of the child Elidyr and his
visit to the fairy realm.

'Others will offer you bribes'
you told Pope Innocent,
'I bring only books.'
No finer epitaph survives
than your own words.
Popes, kings, bishops
and archbishops too,
churches, cities, villages
and castles all shall
crumble into dust but
words and reverence
for words remain,
delight in language,
spoken, written, sung
in Welsh or English
our enduring gift,
rooted so deeply,
woven so firmly
into the fabric
of this land.

BIRD

If you want to be held,
open both your hands.
Rumi

Do not let your strong love pin me down.
Turn it heavenward
and let me fly.

Help me to launch
into that wide, unending sky
where I shall soar
and turning
reach to greet you
when, in the cradle of God's sheltering hands
you too shall launch and fly.

WHAT NEED OF HEAVEN?

What need of heaven if I might find,
one sunny summer morning at my door,
a slender, prick-eared pony
with softest muzzle blowing at my face,
eager to be groomed and saddled,
with easy stride, responsive to
the lightest touch of hand or heel?

What need of heaven if I might ride
the green and quiet roads of Wales,
once trod by Welsh black cattle,
London-bound, iron-shod hooves
clinking on stones the Romans laid
on track ways that the Bronze men knew
and all the folk before?

What need of heaven if we might find
at heat of noon a rowan's shade
and singing mountain brook?
What need of heaven
if I might drowse and hear
my pony's swishing tail
and steady cropping
of the hillside grass
and listen to a buzzard
mewing far above us
in the azure sky?

What need of heaven
if we might find
in lengthening shade
a sheltering cwm
with inn and stable
where we both might
feed and sleep and ride
and sleep and ride again?
What need of heaven then?

SWANSEA REMEMBERED, 1963–1966

For Antonia

It was still Dylan's town – the smell of fish-and-chips,
the raucous gulls, cream-cake shops, pungent cockles,
laverbread, glistening-black, in open, white basins
on the counters of corner shops and
a breeze from the sea.

It was the first town I learned, winding my way to class
past slippered, aproned housewives sweeping steps.
One early summer day I found a steeply-cobbled street.
A rag-and-bone man rattled by, his pony's hooves clip-
clopping and his yodelling cry blended with gull-song
in an azure sky.

I remember the rain, a back-slapping rain cascading on
the roofs of leaky bus shelters, the double-decker buses,
bright-red, splashing to Mumbles through puddles
all along the bay.

And I remember the sea, the wide expanse of it,
the storm-tossed gulls, the oyster-catchers' urgent cries,
the beam of Mumbles' lighthouse swinging
over hurrying waves.

Near to Cwmdonkin Park we looked at digs but found
the house so set about with garden gnomes we fled,
doubled-over, laughing, downhill to Brynmill
just above the sea.

And there, one morning when the tide was high,
we paddled to our classes dodging glass and tar.
And finals done, you cartwheeled a farewell,
slender, bare feet and bright hair tumbling over
sun-bleached grass and like the gulls we dipped
and flew away.

A full, calm tide fills the bay. The huddled town is quiet,
listening for the last, faint, piping of oystercatchers.
One wave lifts, cracks and whispers the length of the bay.
I still hear that sound in my dreams as slowly over
driftwood, seaweed, glass, tar and pebbles
the ebb tide turns.

LESOTHO – FROM KAMPALA

Cloud shadows race
on the bare hills.
Grass scarcely grows.
A keen wind blows
tears to the eyes,
cracks the skin,
buffets the wool
of a starved sheep
stretching, precarious,
for a leaf of willow –
the only green leaf
of a dry spring.
But the air there
is strong and sharp.
It stirs in my memory,
rich with the tang of kraaled cattle,
cow dung fires and the sweet-sickly
smell of warm, home-brewed beer,
crisp with a touch of hoar frost
and smoke-haze blue
over the evening village.

Here, in the lake country,
I am far from the hills
and a moist wind
blows through these memories,
telling of lush foliage,
of dewy daybreaks
and flower-fragrant dusk,
of birdsong at noonday
deep in the flowering tree.
And I rejoice in this
new-found, green Eden,
at this incredible abundance
of blossom, scent and colour,
bird, beast and flower.
Yet, in all this
waving greenness,

I still see
cloud shadows
on the bare hills.

THERE WILL BE MUSIC

There will be music
I heard it as I turned,
feverish,
half-waking,
half-asleep
and lay quite still
astonished by that sound –
far more intricate
than any earthly song.

Never had I heard such
purity, complexity,
such range and tone
interwoven with such
resonance of joy.
It faded as I woke.
I have not heard it since.
But this I know,
though nothing more is clear.
There will be music.

BUT AS FOR ME

But as for me, I will come into Your house
in the multitude of Your mercy
Psalm 5, verse 7

Cool, blue slate tiles
under my bare feet.
Windows opening
onto a sunlit garden,
white muslin curtains
billowing inwards
wafting in birdsong,
scents of mint
and coriander.
Beetroot, damp earth
still clinging to the roots,
and snap peas, just picked,
on the scrubbed wooden table.

Beyond the kitchen
my bare feet find
smooth oak floors
a living-room, a piano,
a deep couch to stretch in,
a window, floor to ceiling
and a writing-table,
pens, pencils and
sheaves of blank,
unused paper.

NOTES

Introduction

Carmarthenshire is so lovely a county it is often called 'The Garden of Wales'. The name Carmarthen is an Anglicisation of the Welsh name Caerfyrddin, which means the 'fort' or castle of Merlin though it is likely that the Myrddin refers to an older Celtic deity.

Mary Stewart, in her retelling of the Arthurian legend, has given an interesting twist to the traditional tale of Merlin's birth. In the opening pages of her first volume, *The Crystal Cave*, she has captured the feel of Carmarthen and the countryside around it so well that whenever I read these pages I am transported back to the place of my birth. There is a hill outside the town called Bryn Myrddin, or Merlin's Hill, but the crystal cave is entirely Mary Stewart's invention.

Dylan Thomas, in his fine short story *A Visit to Grandpa's*, recalled Carmarthen and the Towy estuary as it was in his boyhood when his grandfather lived in Johnstown, a village which was then just outside of Carmarthen.

Pencaer means 'the head of the fort' or citadel, probably a reference to the substantial Iron Age fort on Garn Fawr, the tallest of the hills.

Major Francis Jones, late Wales Herald at Arms, who was born in a village on the coast some miles south of Pencaer, has written these lines in his *Treasury of Historic Pembrokeshire* (Brawdy Books, Pembrokeshire, 1998), now, sadly, out of print:

> . . . Pencaer, promontory of crags, glens and windswept farmlands . . . One does not pass through Pencaer to reach anywhere. For it leads to nowhere. Pencaer is a land's end, girdled by the waves of St. George's Channel, embattled on the landward side by a ridge rising like some grey dragon's back . . .
>
> These high places – there are twenty-one bearing the desription 'carn' – give a special character to Pencaer. Some of the names contain echoes of the Mabinogion and the Age of Saints, while their slopes hold the graves of gold-torqued chieftains of pre-Christian days. (p. 113)

The quotation by Eiluned Lewis is from her book *The Captain's Wife*

(New York, Macmillan, 1943, reprinted in paperback by Honno Classics, 2008).

Preseli

The Preseli Hills rise near to the northern coast of Pembrokeshire and are part of the Pembrokeshire Coast National Park. They are dotted with prehistoric remains and grazed by sheep which are perfectly adapted to the sparse pastures and coarse hill vegetation. They know which part of the hills they belong to and do not wander from it.

'Hefted' is originally a north of England word but I have heard it used in Pembrokeshire.

The word 'pres' or 'prys' means a thicket or woodland. Before the Stone Age all the hills were wooded. 'Seli' or 'Seleu' is a personal name which is tracesd to Salomo or Solomon.

Festival Day

The title of this poem recalls a walk we took during the annual Fishguard International Music Festival which takes place in late July each year.

Garn Barcud means 'the Rock of the Red Kite'. These graceful birds came near to extinction in the twentieth century and had not been seen in Pembrokeshire for many decades but the small population which survived in the hills of mid-Wales is now extending its range and red kites have been seen near to the cottage named after them. I inherited Garn Barcud, a traditional stone farm labourer's cottage, from an uncle in the 1970s. It is our home when we are in Pembrokeshire and is rented out as a holiday cottage when we are not there.

Pwll Strodyr is the name of a tiny cove south of Abermawr on the Pembrokeshire Coast Path. Pwll is the Welsh for pool.

In Nona's Garden

The little river that runs past St David's Cathedral and past Nona's garden is called the Alun. It may take its name from a Celtic river deity, Alauna.

Nona Rees, in whose garden this poem is set, has written in her book *St. David of Dewisland: Patron Saint of Wales* (Gomer Press, 1992, 2008):

All the traditions about the saint agree that he was tall . . . and physically strong: he was able to bear a yoke and pull a plough as well as any team of oxen, yet his diet was mainly bread and herbs. A herb widely used at the time and which formed an important part of the diet of early Christian communities, was watercress . . . David only drank water, and as a self-imposed penance, would stand up to his neck in cold water reciting the psalms.

Penmaen Dewi/St David's Head

For the ancient Greeks, according to their geographer Ptolemy, this headland was the end of the known world.

It was from Whitesands Bay that the Normans launched their infamous invasion of Ireland.

The traditions relate, as Nona Rees has written in her life of St David, that St Patrick wished to found a monastery in St David's 'but was told by an angel that this place was saved for another who would appear thirty years later. The disappointed Patrick was then granted a vision of all Ireland, where his own mission was to be.' In the dunes behind the beach at Whitesands there is a small hillock where there was once a chapel dedicated to St Patrick.

Pen Anglas

'Pen' is the Welsh for a headland or the summit or a hill. There is no known meaning for the word 'Anglas', it is possibly a Norse word in origin. This headland is just to the west of Goodwick, a village just west of Fishguard. There is a ferry crossing from here to Rosslare in Ireland, only fifty miles distant.

Carreg Gwastad is the name of a steep-sided, flat-topped headland on the coast of Pencaer. Carreg means 'rock' while 'gwastad' means "level". This otherwise unremarkable headland is famous as the site of the last invasion of Britain. This happened in February of 1797 when a small flotilla of French warships, manned by fourteen hundred French royalist prisoners, under the command of an American general, William Tate, successfully landed with their supplies on this most inhospitable stretch of coast. The idea behind the invasion was that the Welsh would rise against their English rulers and join with the French in liberating Wales. The local Welsh, who had been watching these ships since they were first sighted off St David's, were, contrary to the invaders' hopes,

Aberbach Cottage

furious at being invaded and outraged when their farmhouses were ransacked and looted by the half-starved French soldiers. The Welsh harassed the invaders, most of whom became severely incapacitated by eating half-cooked chickens and drinking the whisky and brandy with which every farmhouse was well-supplied, either saved from shipwrecks or which had been seized from French merchant ships by Welsh 'privateers', a polite synonym for piracy. The Welsh women joined their menfolk in terrifying the invaders. One formidable local heroine, a sturdy blacksmith named Jemima Nicholas, single-handedly took twelve French soldiers prisoner. By the time the local militia arrived on the scene the invaders were very ready to surrender. The British government of the time kept news of this invasion very quiet as they feared a nationwide panic and a consequent collapse of the national banking system in a time of war.

To mark the bicentenary of this event, and inspired by the famous Bayeux tapestry, almost eighty members of the Pembrokeshire Women's Institutes worked together over a period of three years, 1994–1997, to create a magnificent tapestry in Welsh wool on linen, one hundred feet long and made of thirty-seven individual panels. This is on permanent display in Fishguard Town Hall, across the square from the inn, the Royal Oak, where General Tate signed his surrender. There is detailed information about this now internationally-famous tapestry at the Fishguard tourist information website.

Cemaes Head is the most northerly headland on the North Pembrokeshire coast. The Pembrokeshire Coastal Path begins at Poppit Sands, just to the north of Cemaes Head. The word Cemaes derives from the Welsh word 'camas' which means a bend, inlet or bay. North of Cemais Head the coastline bends inland towards the mouth of the Teifi river and Poppit Sands.

Crincoed means withered woodland. There is a small copse of wind-buffeted trees around these two ruined cottages.

Arriving at Island Farm

Island Farm is not an island but a large, south-sloping headland between Fishguard and Newport. It is separated from the mainland by a marsh with a beach at either end, Pwll Gwaelod facing west toward Fishguard and Cwm yr Eglwys facing east towards Newport. The name Cwm yr Eglwys means the valley of the church. Only the west wall and doorway of this old church remain. The rest of it, together with numerous graves and their contents, was washed away by a great storm in 1859.

It is said that in that one storm one hundred ships were wrecked along the shores of Cardigan Bay, the name given to the whole stretch of sea between Pembrokeshire and the Lleyn peninsula of North Wales.

My mother's sister and her husband farmed Island Farm for thirty years in partnership with my father's second cousin. I spent many weeks there in my teens and early twenties. They had one son, my cousin Thomas. My Aunt Elizabeth was glad of help with house, garden and light farm chores. My Uncle Frank bravely taught me to drive the land-rover. These two winter poems recall the winter I went there to help with the lambing as Uncle Frank had had too close an encounter with the farm boar, resulting in torn tendons on his hand.

Spring Gorse at Aberbach

Aberbach means the small bay. Aber means literally a river mouth, and a stream runs down the wooded valley and into the bay. Garn Barcud is situated in the Aberbach valley. As children, we spent most of our summer holidays in Aberbach Cottage, which was owned by my father's brother, my Uncle Lloyd. He had no children and at his death he generously left the two cottages to me.

In Mute Praise

The name Fishguard is Norse in origin, as is the neighbouring village of Goodwick. These names testify to the Viking presence in Pembroke-shire. They came along this coast, first to pillage but later to settle and intermarry with the local population. There is a history of centuries of trade between Fishguard and the ports of the Hanseatic League on the Baltic Sea.

Morning at Penrhiw

An earlier version of this poem was published in the magazine *Country Quest* in the early 1970s. The name Penrhiw means 'the top of the slope'. This farm is situated at the top of the steep slope above Good-wick. The farmhouse faces south towards Fishguard. 'In Mute Praise' recalls a March morning at Penrhiw. In the Middle Ages Penrhiw was a 'desmene' or manor, comprising much of what is now Goodwick. One branch of my maternal ancestors farmed at Penrhiw in the eighteenth and nineteenth centuries, moving there from Island Farm. The first of them to move wanted to be buried near to the farm he had left. So he left directions for his body to be carried down to a boat in Goodwick. The boat was rowed across to Pwllgwaelod Beach and the coffin was then carried across the marsh to Cwm yr Eglwys where he was buried just by the churchyard gate, thus surviving the great storm that washed so many graves and most of the church out to sea. Until the mid-twentieth century this burial was well remembered as a 'Viking funeral'. In the 1940s Penrhiw was bequeathed to my father, his brother and sister. When my cousin Thomas bought Penrhiw from them in 1971, I spent two months there in the spring house-keeping, cooking and 'go-foring' for him as he began to farm on his own. Springtime at Penrhiw, was for me, after two years of working in drought-stricken Lesotho, an intoxication. I left to work in Uganda as Ann Morgan, Thomas's girlfriend, returned from teaching agriculture in Zambia. The following winter they married. Their welcoming home continues to hold a special place in my heart. Island Farm is now farmed by cousins on my father's side of the family.

In his book *St. David's and Dewisland: A Social History* (Cardiff, University of Wales Press, 1981), David W. James, a former headmaster of St David's County School, wrote:

> The Welsh Land Commission of 1896 commented that it would be difficult to find any other equal area in the United Kingdom where there had been less severance of the old families of owners and occupiers of land. That is still true. Their long associations with these farms – they have played musical chairs with them – and their blood connections and intermarriages are reflected in massive deeds and indentures of contracts. The stranger never fully realises (neither, it is said, sometimes, do they) the extent of the network until the assemblage of relatives come face to face in a funeral. This is the essence of the *llwyth*, the tribal strength, based on land and in which marriage came naturally by arrangement of family and kindred. (p. 55)

At Garn Meini

It has long been assumed that the outcrop of spotted dolerite at the summit of Garn Meini which gives clear evidence of having been worked on by early people was the actual source of the blue stones at Stonehenge. However, very recent research indicates that the source of the Stonehenge blue stones is a site on the northern slope of the Prese-lis. Why these western hills and the spotted dolerite stones they contain were so very special to our early ancestors remains a mystery. The name Meini means 'of stone'.

Hiraeth/Longing for Home

Garn Ingli, a dramatic hilltop of the Preseli Range, rises steeply just behind the town of Newport. The name means The Rock of the Angels. It is said that St Brynach, an early Celtic saint, used to pray and talk with the angels on its summit.

Penysgwarne

The name Penysgwarne means 'the head of the sedge moor'. My father's grandfather, Edward Perkins, bought this farm in 1878, moving there with his six-year-old son, my grandfather. His wife had died when their only child was born. Edward Perkins moved from a farm in St David's Parish where his direct ancestors had farmed for six generations before him. My father inherited Penysgwarne in 1936 from his father. His sister, my Aunt Nesta, lived at Penysgwarne for ninety-six years. We visited her and my grandmother and stayed at Penysgwarne frequently in my childhood. In 1978, after my mother died in Carmarthen, my father and I moved 'home' to Penysgwarne, sharing the house with Aunt Nesta. That same year the Morgan family gave up their tenancy of the farm. My father farmed it for the last eleven years of his life together with my older brother, Edward. At the time of writing Edward and his wife Eireen live at Penysgwarne.

Pen Bwch Ddu probably means 'the headland of the black phantom'. Francis Jones, who listened to and recorded stories told by his elders in the early twentieth century, relates that it refers to a 'bwci' or ghost of a local Welsh chieftain who fled to a cave on a nearby cliff for refuge in the days of Henry VIII when, as the result of a violent feud, the nobles of neighbouring Cemais threatened to kill him and seized his land and cattle. One faithful servant, who was hunchbacked, took provisions to him until his death when this servant buried him in a cleft of the cave. Local people who ventured near this spot on the eve of Michaelmas, the Feast of St Michael, saw a tall cloaked figure on the cliff and at his side his faithful servant.

Garn Falch may be a corruption of Garn Gilfach, named for the farm below it. Garn Fechan means the small hill. Garn Fawr is the large hill.

Messenger of Light

Strumble is a Norse name. There is a lighthouse on a small island off the headland, much needed as these are some of the most treacherous coastal waters in Pembrokeshire.

There Are No Photos

Llanwnda Church is an ancient Celtic foundation dedicated to St Gwnda, an early Celtic saint. He was, it is said, very small of stature but pugnacious in nature. It is said that he fought with another saint over the site of where they both wanted to establish a church and he won. It is also said that the Viking raiders burnt the church twice. The French set it alight during the invasion of 1797, destroying all its early records.

Voices

Tanylan is the name of a farm between Ferryside and Kidwelly in Carmarthenshire. It means 'beside the hill'. One branch of my father's family have farmed there since the middle of the nineteenth century. We made many Sunday afternoon visits to Tanylan.

Manorbier

The opening quotation is from Giraldus Cambrensis, *Itinerary Through Wales/The Description of Wales* (Penguin Classics Series), pp. 150–51.

Elidyr: in his *Itinerary Through Wales*, Giraldus writes down a fairy tale that he heard in St David's. This is the first known written account of a fairy or folk tale about a human child who strayed into the realm of the Tylwyth Teg or Little People.

Swansea Remembered

Brynmill: 'Bryn' means a hill. 'Mill' could be derived from the word 'melin' which means a mill, or from 'melys' which means sweet.

ABOUT THE AUTHOR

Mary Perkins was born and raised in west Wales and is a graduate of the University of Wales, Swansea. She has worked in London, Lesotho, Uganda, Cameroon, Canada and Denmark and now lives with her husband, Richard Gray, in North Carolina.

Mary has published five titles on different aspects of the Bahá'í Faith, its history and teachings, with George Ronald Publisher Ltd. She has also co-authored an introductory book on the Bahá'í Faith with Philip Hainsworth which is popular with readers of all ages and has been published in a third edition in Australia. Some of her work is available in ten languages.

Mary is currently working on a book on storytelling, researching for another biography and continues to write poetry.

www.ingramcontent.com/pod-product-compliance
Lightning Source LLC
LaVergne TN
LVHW091231080426
835509LV00009B/1237